PHIL THE PUG

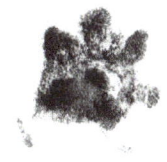

The Puppy Chronicles

Bow down, hoomans! The rise of Phil the Pug starts here!

Phil The Pug

(With help from my Mama, Kaz Rance)

In my own puggy words — I hopes you enjoys my epic first year in this world. It's been a whirlwind of zoomies, belly rubs, and snack-fuelled adventures!

🐾 Phil the Pug 🐾

Scrappy 27/03/2011 – 17/05/2023

🐾 Dedication

This book is for **Scrappy**—our best friend, our loyal shadow, our tiny guardian of love and joy. You were more than just a dog—you were family, you were home, you were the comfort that made every day brighter.

Losing you left a space in our hearts that felt impossible to fill. The grief was heavy, the silence was loud, and our world felt so much smaller without you in it.

But you… you had a plan. You made sure we would be okay. Enter **Phil**—a tiny ball of mischief, joy, and laughter. You knew we needed someone to bring back the smiles, the chaos, the love. And oh, how he did.

Thank you for everything, Scrappy. Thank you for the years of unconditional love, for the memories that will never fade.

We will always miss you. We will always love you. And we will always be grateful for everything you gave us.

🐾 Foreword

From His Mummies

In May 2023, our world changed forever. We said goodbye to our beloved Scrappy, our long-haired Chihuahua, our best friend, our heartbeat in dog form. The grief was indescribable—a sorrow so deep, so consuming, that our home felt empty, as if the very air had lost its warmth.

For weeks, we carried that loss, missing Scrappy's presence in everything—the little sounds, the familiar routine, the way he made every single day brighter.

We were lost. But what we didn't know was that Scrappy had a plan. Because love—true, unconditional love—doesn't end. It transforms. It finds a way.

And that way… was **Phil.**

When we first met Phil, we had no idea that this tiny, wriggly ball of fluff would completely take over our lives.

From the very first zoomie to his hilarious snack treasures, he turned everyday moments into pure entertainment. He wasn't just a puppy—he was a force of nature, a whirlwind of chaos, a master of mischief.

This book isn't just about his first year—it's about the unforgettable journey of raising a pug with more attitude, sass, and charm than should legally be allowed in one tiny body.

But enough from us. Phil has plenty to say for himself.

From Phil the Pug

Ahem.

Let's get something straight.

This book? It's about ME.

I am **Phil**—legend, snack enthusiast, master of zoomies, and the undisputed ruler of my household. I was sent here for a reason. I didn't just show up randomly—I arrived with a mission.

To make my mummies laugh again. To fill the silence with my zoomies. To replace sadness with my signature brand of pug-powered madness. I knew my destiny the moment I set eyes on my Mummies.

From the moment I arrived, I knew these hoomans were mine. I knew my destiny was to take over everything—every blanket, every sofa, every snack within sniffing distance.

This is my story—of how I became a legend, how I trained my mummies to serve me, and how I conquered the hearts of hoomans worldwide.

This book? It's not just about my first year of ruling the household. It's about love—the kind of love that never disappears, the kind that moves from one dog to another, keeping hearts whole, keeping families together.

So, sit back, enjoy the journey, I suggest you **buckle up!**

Welcome to the world of puggy chaos.

I'd like to thank Western Publishing House for all their help and support.

🐾 Introduction

Gather round, hoomans.

I am **Phil**. Master of mischief, ruler of snacks, supreme leader of zoomies, and king of my household.

And this… this is *MY* story.

This book contains everything you need to know about my first year of existence—the victories, the betrayals (mostly bath time), the snack heists, and the outrageous injustice of hoomans denying me second breakfast.

It all started when I arrived on this planet—a tiny, wrinkly, slightly wobbly creature, destined for greatness.

From the moment I met my mummies, I knew I had won the jackpot—two loyal hooman servants, trained in cuddles, belly rubs, and food delivery.

But little did I know, I wasn't just here to live my best pug life…

I was sent on a mission. To restore joy. To bring laughter back into the home that needed it most. To mend hearts with my undeniable cuteness and high-speed zoomies.

It turns out, before me, there was Scrappy—a mighty legend, a beloved companion, a hooman's best friend. His absence left a hole in the hearts of those who loved him.

But Scrappy was wise. He sent me—to fill that space, to bring back the mischief, to remind my mummies that love never disappears… it simply takes on new paws.

And so, I settled into my new kingdom. I claimed every blanket. Every sofa. Every snack within sniffing distance.

I graciously accepted my mummies' and hooman Sister's love, their cuddles, their complete devotion to my puggy greatness. I embraced my legendary spa days—because nothing is more important than puggy hygiene and self-care, thank you very much.

But there was one thing I didn't expect… the betrayal. Not from my mummies. Not from bath time.

From the cats.

These fluffy creatures refused to accept my greatness. They ignored me. They rejected my attempts at friendship. They refused to acknowledge my status as ruler of the household.

I have tried everything—puppy eyes, zoomies, tail wags, diplomatic sniff negotiations, sharing my toys, and my buried treasures (half-eaten snacks). *Nothing works.*

And so, dear readers, I invite you on this journey—my first year of life, of love, of mischief, of snack quests… and of cat-related betrayal.

🐾 Contents:

🐾 Chapter 1: The Grand Arrival

Hello, world! My name is Phil, and I'm an 18-month-old fawn male Pug with an unshakable zest for life! I was born on September 9th, 2023, to my amazing parents—Pumpkin, the most elegant fawn female pug you've ever seen, and Froggo, a dashing black male pug with charisma to spare. My adventure began in a cozy corner of the world, a delightful suburb called Staines-upon-Thames in England, UK. Little did I know, life was about to get a whole lot more exciting when I met my forever family and embarked on the greatest journey ever!

I was one of five adorable puppies born that magical day. Three fabulous females and two marvellous males made up our little crew, each as unique and special as the next.

There was one fawn male (spoiler alert: *that's me!*), two fawn females, one black female pug, and one black male pug. Before I dive into my story, let me introduce you to my siblings. My little sister, Miracle, stayed at our birth home to keep our family entertained with her cuteness. My black pug brother and my fawn sister, Levi and Lexi, found a loving home in North London. They have an amazing life there, and we even stay in touch! I'm secretly hoping for a sibling reunion someday—imagine the chaos!

Now, about my other sister...well, here's the plot twist. I was originally supposed to go to her owner. He said he wanted a male fawn pug like me, but when he came to visit, he saw her and fell head over heels for her instead. Ouch. My little pug heart felt like it had been squished. Why didn't he want me? Was I not cute enough? My tail drooped, and my playful spirit faded for a moment. I couldn't stop wondering—was it my wrinkly face? My big, round eyes? Did I not sparkle like she did? I felt like I was missing some special magic that she had.

But you know what? Life had bigger plans for me, and I'm so glad it did. While I waited for my forever family, life at my birth home was like living in a puggy paradise. Generations of my family surrounded me, and every day was an adventure! Aside from my amazing Mummy, Pumpkin, and my charming Daddy, Froggo, there were other family members: Poppy, my mischievous cousin (she was about eight months old), and Oreo, Zeta, and Luna. The house was bustling with activity, laughter, and endless zoomies. Watching my family play and interact was pure joy. I soaked up every moment, creating memories I'll treasure forever.

Then there was Luna—my wise and wonderful Nanny. She was the first pug puppy the family adopted back in 2017, a striking black pug with a heart of gold. Over the years, she became the matriarch of our family. Luna had her first litter of puppies, which included Oreo and Zeta, my aunts (well, technically Zeta is my aunt—pug family trees can get *very* twisty!). And later, she had another litter that included my incredible Mummy, Pumpkin. Luna's legacy is what brought us all together.

My early days were filled with love, lessons, and laughter, setting the stage for the most exciting chapter of all—finding my forever home. My journey may have started with a little twist, but it led me exactly where I was meant to be.

Growing up surrounded by my family was like starring in the best comedy show ever—a nonstop puggy production filled with love, laughter, and countless misadventures. I'll never forget the first time I opened my tiny eyes to see the world. Everything was brand-new and exciting, like discovering a treasure chest overflowing with squeaky toys. My siblings and I were the ultimate dream team—hours of playing, exploring every corner of our little world, and creating memories to last a lifetime.!

Our days? Oh, they were packed with adventure. From daring chases around our pen to epic wrestling matches, we left no stone unturned in our pursuit of fun. But sometimes, the excitement got the better of us. Picture this: a group of pug puppies so exhausted, we fell asleep...in our food bowls. Yep, food bowls! We were the original champions of food comas, snoozing mid-meal like total pros. It was hilarious, messy, and oh-so-perfectly puggy.

Then there was Poppy, my energetic cousin. She was like the captain of our tiny pug ship, always leading the way and keeping us safe from any imaginary "danger." She was my role model, full of life and always ready for action. Meanwhile, my aunts, Oreo and Zeta, were more like the glamorous sunbathing divas of the family. They spent their days stretched out in patches of sunlight, soaking up warmth like royalty. But when playtime rolled around? Oh, they were quick to join in, bringing their diva energy to our games of tag and zoomie races. It was like having two celebrity guest stars in our little pug sitcom.

And then there was Luna—the wise, nurturing matriarch of the family. She had this incredible calm presence that made you feel safe and loved instantly. Luna was full of stories from her younger days, tales that were equal parts doggy drama and suspense. She'd tell us about her first trip to the park, meeting her best friend (a charming Fox Terrier named Max), and all the wild adventures they had together. Her stories were like bedtime tales, but with an exciting twist that left us hanging on her

every word. We'd sit in awe, imagining ourselves in her paws, facing the world with courage and a wagging tail

As the days went by, my siblings and I noticed something curious—a steady stream of visitors would come to see us. They'd laugh, play with us, and then, one by one, they'd pick one of my siblings to take to their new forever homes. It was bittersweet, really. I was overjoyed for them but couldn't help wondering, *when will it be my turn?* My little puggy heart felt a mix of excitement and nervousness, each day filled with the anticipation of what was to come...

By the time it was just me and my tiny sister Miracle left to be chosen, we'd grown incredibly close. Miracle was so small and delicate—her name was no accident. She was the "miracle pup" everyone was rooting for, and guess what? She made it! Tough, tiny Miracle showed the world what she was made of. We spent endless hours cuddling, playing, and sharing secrets only pug siblings could understand. She was my best friend, my confidant, and my partner in all things mischievous.

Then came the moment that changed everything. My forever family walked through the door and little did I know, destiny had arrived. From the moment I met them, all my worries melted away. Their warm smiles, gentle hands, and soft voices made me feel something I'd never felt before—unconditional love. It was like the universe had been weaving this plan all along, leading me right to them. Suddenly, everything made sense. I wasn't left behind; I was simply waiting for *my perfect match.*

I am, without doubt, the luckiest pug alive!

🐾 Chapter 2: Love at First Wag: The Moment My Forever Began

It was a bright, sunny, crisp Saturday morning in November—the day my life changed forever. My forever family came to meet me, whisking me away to my new home, and they called it my *Gotcha Day*. I mean, how cool does that sound? Like a top-secret mission, with me as the star of the operation! My little pug heart was bursting with excitement, but I'll admit, there was a touch of nervousness too—the kind you feel right before sneaking the last treat from the jar.

The time had come to say my goodbyes. I looked around at my siblings, my pug family, and my human family, knowing this was the end of our chapter together. My human mummy? Oh, she looked like she might cry a river. I mean, can you blame her? Who wouldn't be sad to see this adorable face leaving for new adventures? I was the first of my siblings to go, and if I'm being honest, I think I was her favourite. She gave me extra belly rubs, whispered sweet words, and even sneaked me treats when no one was looking—clear signs of favouritism, right? Not that I'm complaining!

As I strutted out the door, I gave my siblings one last look. "Don't worry, guys," I thought, "I'll send you a postcard from the land of endless treats and belly rubs!" And with that, I embarked on my grand adventure to my forever home.

My new Mummy, being the fabulous human she is, brought along a snazzy red hoody just for me. I mean, talk about style points! Not only did it keep me warm, but I looked absolutely dashing. As if that wasn't enough, she had this magical special blanket that wrapped around her like a hug made just for me. Safe? Warm? Oh yes, I was living the puggy dream.

And then there was the mode of transportation—a fancy Uber Taxi.
Yes, you heard me, I was chauffeured to my forever home like the VIP
pug that I am. Mummy and I were cozied up together in the back seat,
and while the world zoomed past the windows in a blur of excitement, I
tried my best to stay awake. I really did! But the red hoody, the warm
blanket, and my Mummy's gentle cuddles? They teamed up and won.
The next thing I knew, I was out like a light, dreaming of endless treats
and belly rubs.

🐾 Chapter 3: When Paws Met Hearts: Phil's First Encounter with Destiny

Coming into my new home was a day packed with excitement, adventure, and a little puggy tiredness too. After my epic journey, I was buzzing with energy for what lay ahead—new smells, new faces, new everything! As soon as I stepped through the door, I spotted my Mama. I'd met her a week ago, and I instantly remembered her warm hands, big eyes, and that lovely, familiar scent. I knew right then: *this* was home. She scooped me up in her arms, cuddling me close and gently, making me feel like the most special pug in the universe. Mummy, of course, had her phone at the ready and snapped a ton of photos.

We even took our very first selfie together marking the start of my reign as the family's selfie superstar!

When I finally got a chance to explore my new house, I felt like I'd stepped into a gigantic puggy wonderland. Towering furniture loomed over me like mountains, and there was so much space to zoom around. I discovered I had a 12-year-old human sister and—wait for it—*two British Shorthair blue cats*! Oh, they were regal, mysterious, and not sure about me. But hey, I was ready to charm them with my legendary cuteness. No one can resist Phil the Pug, right?

Meeting my human sister was a highlight of my day. She was full of energy, bouncing around and beaming from ear to ear when she saw me. "Phil!" she called out, and oh boy, my tail wagged so fast I thought I might take off like a helicopter! She showered me with cuddles, belly rubs, and non-stop laughter. In that moment, I knew we'd be best friends forever—playmates on all my future adventures!

Now, about those cats. Oh boy, Saffron and Zachary were something else. They acted like royal guards, always watching me with their big, curious eyes.

They moved with such elegance, and let's be honest, they weren't entirely thrilled about my arrival. But did I let that stop me? Not a chance! I couldn't help but want to be their friend. One sunny afternoon, I noticed them playing with their collection of toys. They had everything from feather wands to squeaky mice, and they were having a blast. I thought, "Why not join them?" So, I grabbed a toy and started playing right in the middle of their fun. Chaos ensued. Zach ran off, letting out a meek miaow, while Saffron hissed and attempted to swipe my face with her big paws, claws clenched! I let out a little bark, which sent her scampering up their cat tree, where she glared down at me with a look that could curdle milk!

Then came the pièce de resistance — the lounge. Oh wow! There stood a ginormous plant reaching all the way to the ceiling, covered in sparkling lights and dangling toys. It was mesmerizing! I had never seen anything like it. To top it off, at its base was a soft white blanket that quickly became my new favourite hideout. I heard my parents call it a Christmas Tree. What's Christmas? Why do humans keep trees *inside*? I had so many questions! But for now, I decided to explore its wonders — it was like discovering Narnia!

That day was an unforgettable start to my new life. I already knew this house would be the setting for endless adventures, mischief, and memories to come. From selfies to sibling bonding to cat diplomacy, it was clear: I was home.

Ah, shoes—what a glorious discovery! These marvellous, foot-hugging things humans wear, only to abandon them on the floor as if they're offering them up to me, Phil the Pug, King of Shoe Collectors. If it's on the floor, surely it must be mine. That's just how the rules work in my world, right?

Whenever I spot a lonely shoe just sitting there, I make my move. Stealth mode activated — I'll pounce, grab it between my paws, and trot triumphantly back to my bed with my latest prize. Some shoes are perfect for chewing; they make the most satisfying crunchy sounds (don't worry, I always go for the soft ones). Others? Oh, they're far too precious. Those I simply treasure, guarding them like they're jewels in my puggy kingdom.

The best part, though? Watching my hoomans panic when one shoe mysteriously goes missing. Their frantic dash around the house looking for the other half of their pair? Comedy gold! They'll check under tables, behind curtains, even inside their bags. Meanwhile, I'm just lounging on my bed with their missing shoe tucked proudly under my paw, trying my best not to giggle puggy style.

It's all part of the game, really. I mean, isn't that why they leave shoes lying around? To entertain me? I think I've cracked the code.

When I first arrived at my forever home, my parents gave me the most adorable, snug bed crate—a palace fit for a pint-sized pug like me. It was huge (seriously, I looked like a tiny speck in it), with soft cushioned walls and a matching bed that felt like floating on a cloud. It even had a cosy cover all around, turning it into my own private pug hideout. Sounds perfect, right? Well...not so much.

Don't get me wrong, it was cute and all, but I wasn't into the whole "sleeping alone" thing. Nope! I wanted to be with my parents, where the action—and the cuddles—were. Being shut in made me feel like I was missing out on all the fun. My parents, bless them, tried everything to help me settle. They reassured me it was only for short times while they had "boring human things" to do, and, with a lot of patience and training, I slowly got the hang of it. But let's be real — I had a better plan.

Soon enough, I worked my puggy magic and became their shadow. Wherever they went, I went. And at night? Oh, the grand escape! My crate became a quaint little memory because I took my rightful place—on their bed. It was heaven! So warm, so snuggly, and perfect for a pug like me. They even started dressing me in pyjamas (yes, *pyjamas*), which I must admit, I rocked like a true fashion icon. All those snug vibes and cuddles—I felt like the king of the bed.

And that, my friends, is how I claimed my spot in the most exclusive cuddle club in town.

🐾 Chapter 4: The Great Eye Saga: A Pug's Battle with Adversity

Oh boy, on just my second night in my new forever home, I pulled off a stunt that made everyone gasp! I hurt my precious right eye. Yep, me, Phil the Pug, the Zoomie King, found myself in a situation that was equal parts mysterious and dramatic. Was it the intimidating Christmas tree? A showdown with those stools during one of my legendary zoomie marathons? Or maybe an epic carrot-chomping session gone rogue? The jury is still out, but my family and I agree—it must've been something spectacular!

Let me tell you, it hurt. My eye was throbbing like I'd just lost a round in Pug Wrestling. But did I cry about it? Not a single whimper—because I'm Phil the Brave, of course! My humans were so scared, though. They rushed me to the vet in what felt like a VIP pug ambulance (okay, it was just their car, but I like to exaggerate). The vet said I might lose my eye, which was a serious blow to my plans of winning *Cutest Pug in the Universe*. But I wasn't about to let this setback cramp my style.

The next three months were a whirlwind of medicine, eye drops, and vet visits—basically a pug adventure with a medical twist. I wasn't allowed to go outside for a while, which meant no zoomies, no sniff-fests, and no showing off my dashing looks to the world. A tragedy! But my humans went full-on super-parent mode to take care of me. Honestly, I felt a bit like royalty with all the attention.

Every trip to the vet was like a big city outing. My first rides on public transport? Mind-blowing! Trains and buses are wild, let me tell you. So many humans, so many smells—a symphony of chaos that made my little pug brain spin. People couldn't resist me, of course. They'd stop, say hello, and gush over my charming face (even with a slightly wonky eye). I'd soak up the attention like a sponge until—boom! — nap time hit me. Apparently, I snored so loud that entire buses could hear me. What can I say? When I snooze, I snooze *like a boss*.

Then came the green dye sessions at the vet. Oh, the drama! They'd pop this mysterious dye into my eye, and suddenly, I was a pug with a neon makeover. On the bus ride home, I felt like an intergalactic celebrity. People stared, probably thinking I'd just returned from a pug rave. Thankfully, the glow wore off, and I was back to my usual dashing self—ready to conquer the world one zoomie at a time.

Thanks to my dedicated Mummies, I healed like a champion. No missing eye, no lost charm, just Phil the Pug, ready to take on the world with even more spunk. Now, whenever I look in the mirror, I think, "That's one tough pug staring back at me."

🐾 Chapter 5: My Hoomans, My World: A Pug's Tale of Devotion

After my epic eye injury, my Mummies decided I needed to be kept safe—in a pen. A pen! Like I was some kind of...pet! Okay, I am a pet, but still. I hated it. I couldn't understand why my freedom was being taken away. My Mummy explained it was to protect me while she worked and couldn't keep an eye on me (pun intended). They were worried I might hurt myself again or, even worse, damage my eye to the point of losing it. I guess they had a point, but I wasn't thrilled about my new puggy prison.

Mummy worked from home, so I wasn't totally alone. Mama left every morning at the crack of dawn (6 a.m.—the audacity!) and came back late in the afternoon. My older human sister left for school and didn't return until mid-afternoon. It felt like a *lifetime* waiting for them to come home. Thankfully, Mummy and I spent the day together. She kept me busy, entertained, and even sent adorable photos of me to Mama to keep her updated on my daily pug shenanigans. I was basically the star of a one-dog soap opera.

Now, let's talk about the cats—Saffron and Zachary. Those two had *way* too much freedom for my liking. They would stroll around, tails in the air, acting like they owned the place. Meanwhile, I was stuck behind bars. Sometimes they'd just sit there, staring at me with their judgy little eyes. Naturally, I barked at them to establish my dominance, but that only got me a scolding. "Be kind, Phil. This is their home too," my Mummies would say. Their home? What about my home, huh? It was infuriating!

So, how did I deal with my frustration? Oh, I got creative. I'd tear up my pee-pee mats like a one-pug demolition crew. It was my form of protest, and let me tell you, it was satisfying. But of course, my Mummies didn't appreciate my artistic expression. They'd tell me off while those smug cats watched, probably laughing their little whiskers off. So annoying!

Despite my frustration, I knew my family loved me and just wanted to keep me safe. Plus, I eventually won my freedom back (persistence pays off, folks!). But let's be honest—those cats still owe me for all the judgmental stares. One day, Saffron and Zachary, one day.

🐾 Chapter 6: Phil's Puglic Pee-fection Moment!

So, let me tell you about this bizarre chapter of my life. I had these amazing, magical pee-pee mats at home. They were soft, convenient, and, best of all, private—just how I like it. But then, my mummies had this wild idea: they wanted me to do my business *outside*. Yes, OUTSIDE! In public! Without my trusty pee-pee mat! I mean, can you even imagine? The sheer audacity of it baffled me to my very puggy core. Why on earth would humans want to witness such a... *private moment*? The logic escaped me.

But every day, like clockwork, we'd head out. We'd wander around for what felt like pug years, sniffing every blade of grass and inspecting every lamppost. Sometimes, we'd just stand still—frozen in time—while my mummies cheered me on with, "C'mon Phil, pee-pee! Let's go pee-pee!" As if I didn't hear them the first twenty times. Ugh. Do they think I was born yesterday? No way was I falling for that trick.

Instead, I'd turn it into a game—my game. I'd leap onto benches, do a little victory spin, and give them my most innocent "I-have-no-clue-what-you're-talking-about" face. It was brilliant! But then, one day, Mama went rogue. She brought one of my beloved pee-pee mats and laid it down on the ground! The betrayal! Did she really think I'd stoop to such public embarrassment? Not happening. Not in this lifetime, lady!

Eventually, though, the whole charade got to me. Out of sheer desperation (and okay, maybe to get them to stop begging), I decided to give it a shot. On that fateful day, I did my first-ever pee-pee and poop *outside*. And wow, you'd think I'd just won a puggy Nobel Prize! My mummies went wild—treats, cuddles, the whole shebang. It was a party in my honour! The best part? I made my grand debut in the grounds of a local church. I mean, talk about sacred poop! Even I felt a little proud of myself.

And that, my friends, is how I became Phil the Public Peeing Pro—reluctantly, but with undeniable style.

🐾 Chapter 7: The Royal Bathing Ritual— Phil's Puggy Spa Extravaganza

For some, bath time is a dreaded experience—a battle of wills, a reluctant plunge into the world of cleanliness. But for me? A moment of indulgence. A ceremony of relaxation. A full-fledged puggy spa event worthy of kings.

The signs are clear…

🐾 The murmurs of preparation. 🐾 The gathering of towels and shampoos. 🐾 The unmistakable presence of my puggy spa essentials.

It is time!

My paws, rich in the comforting aroma of popcorn and Doritos, are destined for renewal. My ears, housing a scent so powerful it deserves its own warning label, will soon be cleansed to perfection. My eye bogeys, relentless in their appearance, will finally meet their match.

And I? I am *ready!*

I watch with eager anticipation, my tail wiggling in delight, my eyes shining with excitement. My mummies begin the sacred preparation, adjusting the water, setting the scene. I stand there, full of joy. Majesty. Anticipation.

Then the moment, Mummy cheerfully announcing, "Phil, it's bath time!" I had no clue what that meant, but I was intrigued. They led me to the bathroom, and there it was—a big, shiny tub brimming with warm water and bubbles. It looked like a giant, foamy monster waiting to swallow me whole. Excited? Terrified? I couldn't decide, but I knew one thing—this was going to be *interesting*.

My Mummy gently scooped me up and placed me in the tub. The moment my paws touched the water, I froze. What was this strange, wet stuff? I tried lifting my paws out, but they just kept getting wet again. It was like a never-ending cycle of sogginess! I even thought I might pee-pee right there in the tub—imagine the horror of standing in your own pee-pee, only to have it splashed back onto you. *Yikes!*

As I stood there, bewildered and slightly offended by the wetness, my mummies comforted me. I decided to investigate further and started drinking the water. "Ah, so this is what a bath is—a giant puggy drink!" I thought. My mummies giggled and gently explained that the water wasn't for drinking but for washing. I stared at them, wide-eyed and confused, which they found utterly adorable. Then, the real fun began.

My Mummy lathered me up with doggy shampoo, and suddenly, the bubbles multiplied like magic. Before I knew it, I was transformed into a pug snowman, covered in a mountain of foam. My Mama whipped out her phone and started snapping pictures—paparazzi alert! I tried shaking off the bubbles, but they just kept coming back. It was like a bubble battle I couldn't win, but hey, I looked fabulous.

Then came the rinsing part. My Mummy used a gentle spray to wash off the shampoo, and oh boy, did it tickle! I wiggled, squirmed, and pulled the funniest faces, much to my mummies' delight. They were laughing so hard; I thought they might need a bath themselves. I even managed to splash water all over the bathroom floor—oops! It was a wet and wild adventure, and I was the star of the show. Finally, the bath was over, and my Mummy wrapped me up in a big, fluffy towel. I felt like a snug little pug burrito, ready for cuddles and treats. I was clean, fluffy, and smelled like a field of flowers—irresistible, if you ask me. Turns out, bath time wasn't so bad after all.

And just when you think it couldn't get better… the pampering begins!

The Ear Cleaning: The Peak of Bliss Ohhh… the sweet, sweet joy of an ear rub. My mind drifts into pure relaxation, my body dissolving into comfort. Mummy scratches, cleans, massages, sending me into a trance-like state of euphoria. This is perfection. This is luxury. This is life.

The Dreaded Fold Cleaning: Every Pug's worst nightmare but a necessary interruption! Ah, my beloved folds—the sacred storage units where food, toys, and the outdoors rent space for the day.

But alas… Mummy is relentless. She removes every treasure, wiping away the evidence of past snacking glory. I sigh, I grumble, and I tolerate the injustice because I know… better things are coming.

The Massaging Brush Treatment: A Moment of Indulgence Ohhh, this is the part I LIVE for. The soft bristles glide through my fur, working their magic. I lean into the pure bliss, embracing my spa treatment in full.

The Special Balm: The Final Touch of Pug Beauty *my* nose? Pampered to perfection. My paws? Restored to their soft, princely glory. I admire my own transformation—I am radiant, refreshed, regal.

Ah, the greatest challenge of all. The toothbrush arrives. I know what's coming. I accept my fate—but only on my own terms. My strategy? I chew down on the finger toothbrush. I refuse to let go. They say this is progress—I say it's a battle of wills. But in the end…

I win.

Because progress is progress, and honestly? I'm just here for the attention and snacks afterward.

And so, the ritual ends—I emerge from this grand transformation, clean, refreshed, smelling like a civilized creature and elevated! I strut, showing off my refreshed puggy beauty, my soft paws, my radiant nose.

And my mummies? They admire their work. And yet… I know that soon, my paws will return to their snacky scent, my folds will reclaim their mystery treasures, and my mummies… They will never escape the endless cycle of cleaning and puggy maintenance...

Because I am Phil—Master of Mischief, Supreme Judge of Hygiene Betrayal, Ultimate Pug Spa Enthusiast, **Supreme Ruler of Bath-Time Bliss, and Undeniable Pug of Perfection.**

Chapter 8: The Pug Warrior vs The Cleaning Monster

Ah, the day I met *The Cleaning Monster*—a moment of pure terror and eventual triumph in my puggy life! It all started one fateful morning when my Mummy opened the cupboard door to retrieve something big, and cumbersome, and I had no clue what it was, but I was about to find out...and I wasn't prepared.

Out it came—a big, shiny, growling beast with a long, wriggly hose. To a tiny pug like me, it looked like something straight out of a nightmare. My heart skipped a beat as I watched in disbelief. Then, she plugged it in and turned it on. The noise! Oh, the *noise!* It was like thunder on steroids, and I was convinced my puggy ears might just pop off. I tried to summon every ounce of courage in my fluffy little body, but nope—bravery? Out the window. I bolted to the nearest corner and hid behind the sofa, peeking out with wide, terrified eyes to see what this monstrous contraption was plotting. My family? Oh, they found the whole thing hilarious. Apparently, trembling paws and a quivering pug face are "adorable." Not for me, they weren't!

As the Vacuum Cleaning Monster crept closer, I couldn't take it anymore. I let out a soft, pitiful cry—my desperate plea for rescue. Thankfully, Mummy noticed my distress and turned off the roaring beast. She scooped me up, wrapped me in cuddles, and reassured me it was just a machine and not, in fact, a pug-eating monster. I wasn't fully convinced, but her hugs did help a little.

But this wasn't the end of our saga. Oh no, my Mummy decided it was time for me to face my fear head-on. She placed me on the floor, turned the monster back on, and held me close so I could observe it from a safe distance. I glared at it suspiciously, but as I watched, I started to realize...it wasn't *attacking* anyone. Just a noisy, annoying thing cleaning the house. Huh.

Over the next few days, I got braver and braver. Eventually, I turned the tables—I became Phil the Brave, Defender of the Living Room! Whenever Mummy would vacuum, I'd bark and chase the beast around, pretending to be a fearless pug warrior. My family loved it, cheering me on as I showed the monster who's boss. Honestly, I kind of enjoyed the attention.

In the end, I conquered my fear of the Vacuum Cleaning Monster. It became just another part of our daily routine, and I even grew to find it amusing. Sure, it's still loud and obnoxious, but now I see it for what it truly is: a big, shiny, slightly overdramatic cleaning machine. And nothing, not even the noisiest monster, can outshine Phil the Fearless!

🐾 Chapter 9: 🎄 Paw-lidays & Celebrations: A Pug's Guide to Festive Madness

It was Christmas Eve! What was Christmas? I had absolutely no clue—but boy, I could feel the electric energy buzzing through my house. My family was bustling around like elves in a toy workshop, laughing, decorating, and prepping for what felt like the *biggest event in pug history*. I soaked up every ounce of their excitement, and my little pug heart raced with joy.

And not forgetting — the grand, glittering plant they called a "Christmas Tree." Oh, it was magnificent! Shiny baubles dangled from the branches like sparkling puggy treasures. Twinkling lights danced around it, casting magic across the room. And guess what? It even had toys hanging from its branches! My zoomie paws couldn't resist running circles around it and diving under the fluffy white blanket at its base. It was like my own enchanted puggy hideout—a winter wonderland fit for a Pug king.

As evening rolled in, my family gathered in the living room wearing their cozy pyjamas. And guess what? I got to wear *my* very own Christmas outfit! They transformed me into Puggy Claus himself, complete with festive vibes and snuggliness. I felt like the VIP of Christmas. My family started telling stories about someone called Santa Claus—a jolly fellow who apparently sneaks down chimneys and leaves gifts for everyone. *Gifts?* For me too? Suddenly, Christmas sounded like the best idea in the world.

After dinner, we all piled onto the *humongous* sofa near the tree. My family picked a Christmas movie, and we laughed, snuggled, and sang along to the music (okay, they sang—*I* barked along in harmony). They couldn't stop giggling as I tried to hit all the high notes. Clearly, I was the showstopper of the night.

As bedtime approached, my family explained something very important—Santa only visits if everyone is asleep. My puggy ears perked up. Santa? Coming here? I didn't want to miss him! But the day's excitement had worn me out, and I couldn't fight the sleepiness creeping in. They tucked me into their cozy bed with my favourite toy, and I closed my eyes, dreaming of jingling bells and presents galore.

Just as I was drifting into puggy dreamland, I heard a faint *jingle*. Was I imagining things? I shot up, wide-eyed, and raced downstairs. There, near the shimmering Christmas Tree, was a shadow—and then I saw him! It was Santa! The legend himself! He was placing presents under the tree, including a special one just for me. I wagged my tail furiously, but I stayed quiet (can you believe it?) so I wouldn't scare him away. Santa Claus in my house—it was like meeting a celebrity!

Christmas Eve was pure magic, and I couldn't wait to see what Christmas morning had in store. I knew one thing for sure—this holiday was officially pug-approved!

Christmas Day! Wow, I had no clue what this day was all about, but the excitement was practically bouncing off the walls—and me, of course. My little pug heart couldn't handle it! I woke up bright and early with my family, and we were still rocking our cozy pyjamas as we dashed downstairs. The lounge was glowing with festive vibes. The Christmas

Tree stood tall and proud, twinkling away like the star of the show. And oh, the presents! Piles of colourful boxes and bags surrounded it, practically calling my name.

As my family gathered around the tree, the great unwrapping began. *Rip, tear, squeak!* It was chaos, but the best kind of chaos. Then it happened—the moment of puggy destiny. They handed me a special present with MY NAME on it. I wagged my tail so fast it practically created its own breeze. I tore into the wrapping paper like a tiny tornado. Inside? A squeaky toy shaped like a reindeer! A REINDEER! I mean, come on, could anything be better? I squeaked it, tossed it, and made it the star of my puggy antics. My family couldn't stop laughing, showering me with cuddles and cheering me on. They handed me even more presents—more toys, more treats, and oh my pugness, more squeaky joy. Santa Claus? You're officially my hero.

But then... *sniff sniff.* What was that heavenly smell? My puggy nose went into overdrive. Delicious aromas wafted through the house as my Mummy worked her magic in the kitchen. Turkey? Stuffing? Yummy treats? My mouth watered so much, I might've drooled a little. Okay, maybe a lot. I stationed myself in the kitchen, throwing my best puppy eyes in hopes of scoring a taste of the feast. And guess what? They shared! I got my very first bite of turkey and let me tell you—it was life-changing. Turkey officially holds a special place in my puggy soul.

The rest of the day was a whirlwind of fun. We played games, laughed until our sides hurt, and soaked in the festive joy together. I joined in the games, barking and zooming around like the life of the party. At one point, I might've stolen someone's trainer... but hey, it's Christmas, right? All rules are off!

As the day wound down, I sat cuddled with my Mummies, feeling warm and loved. It wasn't just the presents or the treats—it was the magical feeling of togetherness that made it the best Christmas Day ever. My puggy world was glowing with happiness, and I couldn't wait to see what adventures the next festive celebration would bring.

Oh, and just when I thought the fun was over, they introduced me to *another* exciting day—New Year's Eve. A day with even more fun and mischief waiting for me.

🐾 Chapter 10: A Pug's New Year Resolution: More Snacks, More Naps, More Zoomies

New Year's Eve—the night of sparkle, excitement, and a whole lot of puggy fun! The evening started with my family bustling around the house like a pack of cheerful elves, getting everything ready for the big celebration. And then, it happened—they dressed me in a *tiny tuxedo*. Oh yes, a tuxedo! I mean, talk about sophistication.

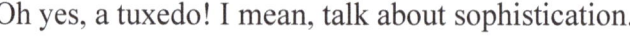

I strutted around like a movie star on the red carpet, stopping to admire myself in the mirror. "Who *is* that handsome devil?" I thought. My family couldn't stop taking pictures, and honestly? I was living for the attention. Puggy paparazzi alert!

The house was buzzing with festive vibes. The flashing disco lights alongside the shimmering Christmas Tree created this magical, dazzling atmosphere. Naturally, I couldn't contain my excitement—I zoomed around like a rocket, weaving through furniture and wagging my tail like it had a mind of its own. It was almost too much fun.

As the night unfolded, my family gathered in the living room for maximum merriment. We watched movies, played silly games, danced like no one was watching, and laughed until our sides hurt. I joined in with my signature pug bark, adding my own musical flair to the festivities. My family found my enthusiasm hilarious, showering me with cuddles between rounds of games. If puggy dancing isn't the life of the party, I don't know what is!

Then came the grand finale—the countdown to midnight! Excitement filled the air as we crowded around the TV to watch the fireworks display. Let me tell you, fireworks are wild. When those colourful explosions lit up the sky, my eyes widened to the size of saucers. The crackling sounds? They made me bounce on the spot in astonishment. I was equal parts amazed and confused by this glowing, noisy spectacle.

The fireworks outside the house added a real-life touch of magic, and I couldn't stop staring.

Finally, the clock struck midnight—**HAPPY NEW YEAR!** My family erupted into cheers, hugging each other and, of course, smothering me in kisses and cuddles. I was officially crowned "Most Loved Pug of the Year" (well, in my head). We all snuggled up together by the glowing Christmas Tree, watching the fireworks paint the sky in vibrant colours. It was beautiful, chaotic, and downright unforgettable.

In summary, my very first Christmas and New Year—what a whirlwind of chaos, wrapping paper destruction, and turkey-fuelled joy! The house practically burst with festive magic, and I, Phil the Pug, was smack dab in the middle of it all.

Most of all, my little puggy heart was full—with cuddles, laughter, and the pure magic of spending the holidays with my humans. Luckiest pug in the world? Absolutely.

🐾 Chapter 11: New Year, Same Pug: Phil's Manor is Born!

Now let's talk about the very first day of 2024. New Year's Day, they called it—a whole new adventure waiting to unfold! My family had a brilliant plan: a trip to this enormous, magical place I would later crown as *Phil's Manor Park*. A place so majestic, it could only be named after yours truly. Spoiler alert: it was a day packed with thrills, zoomies, and more snacks than I ever dreamed possible.

The day began with excitement buzzing through the house. My parents bundled up in their coats, and I wiggled into my trusty harness. Let me tell you, I felt like an adventurer preparing for the expedition of a lifetime. When we arrived at the park, my jaw nearly dropped (if that's even possible for a pug). This place was HUGE! Trees taller than I'd ever seen, paths winding in every direction, and smells—oh, the smells! My puggy senses were tingling, and my paws itched to explore.

First stop: the small children's play area. Swings swayed, slides gleamed, and climbing frames towered like castles. I watched the kids run around, laughing and playing with boundless energy. Honestly, they were kindred spirits. I wanted to dive right in and join their games, but my family gently reminded me it was *for children only*. Humph. So, I sat on the sidelines, wagging my tail so hard it could've powered the swings.

Next up: picnic time! My family unpacked the most delicious-smelling feast at one of the picnic tables. The sunshine warmed our fur (and hair for the humans, of course) as we enjoyed the beautiful surroundings. My nose twitched as the aroma of toasted sandwiches filled the air. Did I score a taste? You bet I did! A tiny bite of sandwich bliss later, and my tummy and I were in heaven.

The adventure didn't stop there. We strolled over to the cafes, where the crowds were brimming with friendly faces—and friendly hands ready to give me cuddles! I soaked up every bit of the attention like a sponge. Then, the pièce de résistance: cake. My Mummies shared a tiny piece with me, and let me just say, *cake is officially life.*

But the real showstopper? The *Manor House*. Oh, wow! This place was breathtaking—grand architecture, colourful gardens, and pathways that seemed to stretch into forever. I raced around the gardens, sniffing every flower like a professional floral inspector. They smelled incredible, and I might've sneezed once or twice from sheer delight. My family couldn't stop snapping pictures, and I felt like a bona fide celebrity.

And just when I thought the park couldn't get any better, we found the *green parks*. Two enormous fields of open space! Imagine it—room to run, tumble, and roll as far as my little legs would carry me. I bolted like lightning, feeling the wind ruffle my fur. Other dogs joined in for zoomie races, and we frolicked like old friends. Grass? Rolling in it is one of life's simplest yet greatest joys.

By the time we headed home, my paws were tired, my belly was full, and my heart was bursting with happiness. The park wasn't just a magical place—it was my new kingdom of adventure. Phil's Manor Park was officially pug-approved.

🐾 Chapter 12: Mount Staircase: A Pug's Epic Climb!

Now, let me set the record straight: to a tiny pug like me, those stairs weren't just stairs. Oh no, they were a terrifying, towering mountain—a Mount Everest of doom! Sure, I could zoom *up* those steps like a rocket-powered ninja, but coming *down*? That was an entirely different ballgame. Those big, scary steps stretched on forever, and let me tell you, I was convinced they were plotting against me.

It all began when I was about three months old, a wee little pug full of curiosity and mischief. One fine day, I discovered the thrill of running *up* the stairs. It was pure exhilaration! I felt like a hero in an epic adventure movie. Up I went, my little legs pumping with determination, reaching the top in no time. I stood there, chest puffed out, surveying the kingdom below like the king of the world. But then, disaster struck. I peered over the edge, and the stairs glared back at me. My confidence crumbled faster than a dropped biscuit. *How on earth was I supposed to get down?*

And so, there I sat at the top of the stairs, frozen in fear, letting out my soft, heart-wrenching cry. "Help meeeee! I'm stuck!" I whimpered, sounding like a puppy in a soap opera. My Mummies would hear my dramatic pleas, and soon enough, my loyal rescue team would arrive. With chuckles and loving smiles, they'd scoop me up and carry me back to the safety of solid ground. My dignity may have taken a hit, but boy, was I relieved.

This became my routine for months. I'd charge up the stairs like a champion, only to stage my very own dramatic damsel-in-distress act at the top. My family thought it was hilarious. I mean, *they* weren't the ones facing the stair-monsters! But at least they always rescued me with laughter and cuddles.

Then, one fateful day when I was about five months old, I decided enough was enough. It was time to conquer the beast once and for all. I stood at the top of the staircase, puffed out my chest, and gave myself the pep talk of the century. *"You've got this, Phil. You're not just any pug—you're THE Phil!"* With a deep breath, I placed one paw on the first step. It wobbled like the floor of a haunted house, but I pressed on. Slowly, carefully, one step at a time, I made my way down, my tail wagging with determination.

"Come on, Phil! You can do it!" Mama cheered, her voice full of encouragement.

With every step, I felt more confident. I was doing it! I was really doing it! Finally, my paws touched the bottom step, and I gazed back up at the once-mighty staircase. My family erupted in applause, cheering as if I'd just won Olympic gold. In that moment, I felt like a true hero. No, scratch that—a legend!

From that day on, the staircase and I had a truce. I could zoom up and down with the grace of a squirrel on a sugar rush, and fear was a thing of the past. My family still laughs about my early stairway antics, but hey, every great hero starts somewhere, right? I emerged from that ordeal a braver, bolder, and slightly sassier pug.

The staircase? Conquered. Phil? Victorious.

🐾 Chapter 13: My Quest for Feline Friendship!

I've always been fascinated by the two British short hair blue cats, Saffron and Zachary, who live with me. They look so cool and regal, and I just want to be their friend. But for some reason, they don't seem to like me very much. I don't get it! I'm friendly and fun, and I just want to play with them.

One sunny afternoon, I saw Saffron and Zachary lounging on their fancy cat sofas. They looked so comfy, and I thought, "Why not join them?" So, I trotted over and plopped myself right in the middle of Saffron's favourite spot. She let out a loud whine and miaowed at me, and Zachary hissed. But I didn't mind. I just wanted to be close to them.

Then, I noticed the towering cat tree in the corner of the living room. The cats climbed it so easily, and I thought it might be the perfect way to get their attention. With all my energy, I tried to climb the cat tree. My little paws struggled to find a grip, and I ended up dangling from one of the lower shelves. The cats watched me with wide eyes, probably thinking, "What is this pug doing?" But I was determined to make it to the top.

Despite their protests, I kept trying to be their friend. I would sneak onto their cat sofas when they weren't looking, curling up and pretending to be one of them. They would whine and miaow, but I would just wag my tail and give them my best puppy eyes. I hoped they would eventually see that I just wanted to be friendly.

One evening, I tried to climb the cat tree again. I lost my balance and tumbled to the floor. Saffron and Zachary watched in horror, but I quickly got up, shook myself off, and gave them a big, cheeky grin. They couldn't help but be amused by my antics. Maybe, just maybe, they were starting to see that my heart was in the right place.

My quest for feline friendship is a never-ending adventure. I might not have won them over completely, but my determination and friendly nature are undeniable. And who knows? Maybe one day, Saffron and Zachary will realize that having a pug as a friend isn't so bad after all. I think Saffron is slowly coming around to the idea, as she has started to sit near me.

🐾 Chapter 14: Chocolate, Chaos, and Cats: An Easter to Remember!

Ah, Easter—a day filled with the promise of treats, surprises, and a bunny who apparently delivers presents. What a time to be alive for a pug! My first Easter was nothing short of extraordinary, with a mix of excitement, mischief, and just a touch of feline drama.

The morning started with a mysterious visit from this so-called *Easter Bunny*. I didn't see him myself (slippery fellow), but boy, did he leave behind the loot! My family gathered around to reveal the stash of colourful goodies, and guess what? There was a special surprise just for me: a dog-friendly chocolate Easter egg! Let me tell you, that thing smelled *amazing*. My tail went into full helicopter mode as my Mummies handed it to me.

Now, I may have been a pug newbie when it came to Easter eggs, but I wasn't about to let that stop me. My little paws got to work, nudging and rolling the egg around the floor like a pro. I was determined to crack that thing open and get to the good stuff inside. The only problem? I might've gone a bit overboard. My egg rolled… and rolled… and rolled—straight into the path of Saffron and Zachary, the household's regal (and slightly grumpy) feline overlords.

Let's just say, they weren't amused. Saffron shot me a death glare that could curdle milk, while Zachary dramatically swished his tail and huffed away in protest. Honestly, I think they were jealous of my egg. I mean, who wouldn't be? My family, however, found the whole scene hilarious. They cheered me on as I chased my runaway egg across the room, looking like a tiny pug on a mission.

Finally, after much rolling, pawing, and a small tug-of-war with a rug, I managed to crack the egg open (with a little help from Mummy). The taste? Oh, it was heavenly! My first taste of dog-friendly chocolate was an experience I'll never forget. It was sweet, rich, and everything my little pug heart had ever dreamed of.

The rest of the day was a blur of cuddles, playtime, and more Easter surprises. My family had hidden more treats around the house, and I spent the afternoon sniffing them out like a pint-sized treasure hunter. Each discovery was met with cheers, belly rubs, and maybe just a tiny bit more chocolate.

As for Saffron and Zachary? Well, let's just say they spent the day perched on their cat tree, looking down on me like I was the court jester of the kingdom. But hey, not everyone can appreciate the joy of rolling an Easter egg across the floor, right?

My first Easter was a celebration of fun, food, and the undeniable truth that every holiday is better when you're surrounded by love (and snacks). I might've caused a bit of chaos, but that's just part of the Phil experience. Here's to many more egg-citing adventures!

🐾 Chapter 15: Phil the Pug: Fashion Icon Extraordinaire!

Well, hello world! It's me, Phil the Pug—a little ball of adventure, charm, and now… wait for it… fashion royalty! That's right, I've officially become the face of fabulous dog accessories as a brand ambassador for none other than the amazing **Mylo & Mas Boutique**. Cue the confetti, folks, because this is a *dream come true*.

Let me spill the beans on how it all started. Picture it: April 2024, the sun shining, my tail wagging, and the exciting news that my Instagram buddy, Mylo—a super cool three-year-old male fawn pug—and his amazing Mamas, Martina and Michaela, wanted *me* to join their fashion squad. Mylo & Mas Boutique, based in the gorgeous land of Galway, Ireland, is all about chic, stylish dog accessories. Harnesses collections? Stunning. Pom-pom necklaces? Adorable. Special ID Tags? You got it! And guess what? I get to try them *all* and strut my stuff for the world to see.

Being a brand ambassador is, in a word, *epic*. Imagine this: a new parcel arriving at the house—it's like Christmas morning every time! My tail wags so furiously, I swear it could generate enough wind power to fuel a small town. Mama opens the package, and inside is pure accessory gold—a shiny harness, a matching lead, my own name on a tag, epic, a poop bag with style (yes, really), and sometimes even a pom-pom necklace. I put them on, strike a pose, and suddenly, I'm not just Phil the Pug—I'm Phil, the fashion icon.

Now let me tell you about the photo shoots. Oh, the photo shoots. Hours of posing, tail wagging, and finding my *good side*. It's hard work being this adorable, but someone's got to do it. Mama takes picture after picture, and I bask in the spotlight like the true star I am. And when I see those pictures online, showcasing my glamorous new looks? I feel on top of the world.

But here's the best part: I'm not just a model—I'm part of something truly special. Mylo & Mas Boutique is a small business with a big heart, and being one of their ambassadors fills my puggy soul with pride. I'm humbled to represent them, and I can't wait for the day I travel to Galway to meet Mylo and his Mamas in person. Just imagine the mischief and fun we'll get up to!

So, if you ever spot me rocking a fabulous harness or a cute pom-pom necklace, know that I'm doing it with pride, joy, and a whole lot of love. I'm Phil, the pug with a passion for fashion, and I promise to keep bringing smiles, wagging tails, and timeless style to the world. Stay tuned, folks—this fashion adventure is just getting started. Life's always better with a little pug sparkle, after all!

🐾 Chapter 16: The Crown Jewels Chronicles: Phil's Epic Vet Adventure!

Ah, what a glorious morning it was! I woke up with the excitement of adventure bubbling in my little puggy soul. Today was going to be amazing—I could *feel* it. Mama and I got ready to head out, and while I noticed breakfast was suspiciously absent (*ahem*), I was too busy wagging my tail to care. Adventure awaits!

We set off into the cool May morning, crossing the busy road (I strutted like a pug with a mission, of course) and arrived at the bus stop. And then—jackpot! The bus stop was bustling with schoolchildren, and oh, did they love me. *"Look at the cute pug!"* they said, while my tail wagged at supersonic speed. I soaked up the attention like the star I am, and when the bus finally arrived, the kids even sat near me, chatting and laughing. I was practically their mascot. When we reached their stop, they waved and said goodbye. I felt like royalty, bidding my subjects farewell.

Mama and I continued our journey, trekking to another bus stop. This time, the crowd was big, the bus was late, and when it finally rolled up… it was full! *Excuse me?* What kind of adventure denies entry to a VIP like me? Mama and I waited and waited, but I think the bus gods were against us. So, she decided to call an Uber Taxi. Enter: The Uber Man.

The Uber Man was lovely—like, really, lovely. He spent the entire journey talking about his own dog, while I nodded along wisely, as if to say, *"Yes, I understand the struggles of dog parenthood. It's exhausting but rewarding."* I could tell he was charmed by my presence (who wouldn't be?), and before I knew it, we arrived at our destination: the dreaded vet.

Now, let me tell you something about vets—they're sneaky. With soft words and reassuring pats, they lure you in. Mama was calm and sweet, whispering little reassurances as we walked inside. But something felt *off.* My puggy senses were tingling. When we checked in at reception, the kind vet appeared and tried to lead me away. Excuse me, lead me *WHERE?*

Reluctant doesn't even begin to describe my reaction. I froze. My paws were glued to the floor. *"Nope, no way, not today!"* But then Mama gave me a big cuddle, and I decided to be brave. I waddled in with the kind vet (I knew them, so at least there was some trust there). I followed Mama dutifully, but the moment I saw her wave goodbye, my puggy heart dropped. *Wait, where's she going?* I reluctantly followed the familiar vet, glancing back at the door with my big, soulful eyes. This was the beginning of the unknown.

What happened next was a blur. One moment I was awake, and the next I was in dreamland, snoozing through mysterious happenings. When I finally stirred, I was greeted by kind voices and gentle hands. The vets were so lovely, whispering sweet reassurances and offering pats galore. They even took photos of me—because obviously, I'm pug-perfection, even post-operation!

But as I stretched and blinked my sleepy eyes, I noticed something... odd. My private area felt a little sore, and I couldn't quite figure out why. *Had I been in a battle? Was I now a war hero?* The vets didn't spill the details, but they kept saying things like, *"You're such a brave boy, Phil!"* I decided to roll with it—after all, bravery is my brand.

However, confusion set in. My little body felt funny—there was a strange soreness in my private area—and I couldn't figure out why. And worse than that? Mama and Mummy were *gone*. My puggy heart sank as the thought crossed my mind: *Had they abandoned me? Had I done something wrong? Was I no longer wanted?*

My sadness was palpable. I looked around the room, searching desperately for their familiar faces. My tail was still, my usually waggy spirit dimmed by the fear that I'd been sent away. But then the kind vets stepped in, whispering sweet reassurances and offering gentle pats.

They told me how brave and adorable I was and took lots of photos, which I'll admit felt a bit flattering—even amidst my despair. Then I heard it—the familiar sound of Mama's voice on the phone. The vets were telling her that everything had gone well. Relief washed over me. *Mama and Mummy know I'm okay,* I thought, letting out the smallest, cutest sigh (because yes, even my sighs are adorable).

I cannot tell you the relief which began to wash over me. *Mama and Mummy hadn't abandoned me,* I realized. *They know I'm okay.*

Soon enough, Mummy and Mama returned to retrieve me. Ah, much to my puggy horror, they didn't stop at compliments and kind pats—they came armed with *accessories*. Yes, accessories! Before I could even say, *"Excuse me, I'm au naturel,"* they dressed me in this so-called special surgical vest. Sure, it was giving haute couture meets doggy ER, but comfort? Let's just say it wasn't exactly my style. I gave them my best side-eye of disapproval.

But oh, the indignity didn't end there. They then had the audacity to present… a carrier. *A carrier?!* As in, *a box for lesser creatures who aren't me?* Do they even *KNOW* who I am? I made my feelings crystal clear—wiggles, grunts, and the full pug protest package. Ultimately, they relented (as they should!) and carried me like the royalty I am. With gentle hands and whispered apologies, they cradled me in their arms. Honestly, sometimes you just must remind the humans of your worth.

I mean, can you even imagine it? The drama, the betrayal, and yet… I carried myself with grace. Such is the life of Phil, fashion-forward and always dignified. Or at least, I try. 🐾

We got into another Uber—a wonderful driver who couldn't stop chatting about his dog. By the time we reached home, I was starting to feel like myself again. The vets had warned Mama and Mummy that I'd be sleepy and tired, but oh, how wrong they were. I couldn't help but snigger internally. Rest? Me? Oh, they had no idea who they were dealing with. The second my paws hit home turf; I was reborn. Zoomies! Sofa leaps! Bed bounds! Mama and Mummy watched in shock as I displayed my trademark energy, as if to say, *"Crown jewels or not, I'm still Phil the Fearless!"*

Heroic? Absolutely. Mischievous? Always. My vet adventure was a saga of bravery, confusion, and ultimately, puggy triumph. So, bow down, humans, because I am Phil, the indomitable adventurer who took on the vets and emerged victorious - with or without my royal jewels!

Bow down, humans, for I am Phil, the fearless adventurer!

🐾 Chapter 17: Phil's Merseyside Mischief!

Ah, Liverpool! A city of adventure, treats, and—most importantly—celebration. But before we get to the magical party, let me take you on the thrilling rollercoaster that was my journey to this lively destination. Buckle up, humans, because it's going to be paws-itively entertaining!

It was a warm June morning, and chaos was unfolding around me. My family was darting about the house like frantic squirrels, packing luggage, forgetting things, and mumbling about schedules. As for me? I calmly supervised (read: sat in the middle of everything, occasionally pawing the bags for good measure). Finally, after saying goodbye to Saffron and Zachary—who couldn't care less that we were leaving—we set off. Destination: Liverpool!

First stop: the bus to the tube station. Let me tell you, the excitement bubbling in my little puggy soul was off the charts. The tube into London? Oh, it was a bustling wonderland! People everywhere, feet shuffling, bags rustling—pure chaos. But the best part? The attention. I soaked it up like sunshine on a cold day. "Aw, look at the cute little pug!" they said. I wagged my tail and gave them my best puppy-dog eyes. It was working. My charm is truly unstoppable.

Next up, London Euston Station—a place filled with trains, humans, and snacks (mostly snacks, as far as I was concerned). We boarded a super-fast train to Liverpool, and oh boy, was it packed. People squeezed into tiny seats, bags everywhere, and the temperature? Hotter than the sun, I swear! I found myself a cozy spot, curled up, and drifted into dreamland. I snored a little (okay, maybe a lot), much to the passengers' delight. They smiled and giggled—I'm a traveling entertainer, apparently.

After almost 3 hours, we finally arrived in Liverpool Lime Street Station. Cue excitement! And thank pugginess to get off this puggy hot train! Waiting for us were Nanny Sue and Grandad John, my mummy's lovely parents. They greeted us with hugs, smiles, and—best of all—cuddles for me. As if that wasn't enough, they whisked us away to McDonald's for a treat. Chicken nuggets, folks. *CHICKEN. NUGGETS.* My taste buds did a happy dance. Life doesn't get better than a nugget feast.

The next stop was Nanny and Grandad's house—a place filled with love, warmth, and more excitement than my little pug heart could handle. The garden? Stunning! Flowers everywhere, trees towering above me, and grass that was practically begging for zoomies. And the highlight? Grandad John, the genius, made me my very own swimming pool! It was hot, I was cooling off, and suddenly I decided Grandad was officially the greatest human on the planet.

Then came the main event: Nanny and Grandad's 50th wedding anniversary celebration. Let me tell you, this was a party to remember. I met SO many people—Mummy's siblings, nieces, nephews, cousins. It was like meeting my extended royal family. But the drama? Oh yes, the Cockapoo chaos. Two female Cockapoos (who clearly didn't understand the concept of personal space) spent the evening trying to sniff my bot-bot. *Excuse me, ladies!* Not to mention their audacious attempt at stealing food from the humans' table. Thankfully, they were caught and given a stern talking-to. Justice for pug kind prevailed.

The evening was filled with laughter, music, and, of course, food. Oh, the food. My very own doggy cake—special, sweet, and utterly delicious. My tummy was in heaven, and my heart was full. It was a magical celebration of love, family, and, let's be honest, how adorable I am.

As the day drew to a close, I curled up with my family, reflecting on my grand Liverpool adventure. I'd braved the journey, charmed the humans, survived the Cockapoo sniff-off, and eaten nuggets and cake. A small pug in Liverpool, but a mighty adventurer in spirit. Here's to more grand journeys ahead!

🐾 Chapter 18: Confetti, Chaos, and Cats: Mama's Surprise Birthday Bash!

It all started on an impossibly hot June morning. I woke up, ready for adventure, and bounded down the stairs with Mummy. As we entered the lounge, I was greeted by an explosion of colour—balloons, banners, and decorations galore! My little puggy heart swelled with excitement. Was this breathtaking spectacle all for me? Finally, my family had recognized my true place as the centre of the universe, right?

But alas, Mummy broke the news—it wasn't for me. *What?!* It was Mama's birthday, and we were throwing her a surprise party. While I was a little disappointed, I quickly rallied. After all, I love a good party. I volunteered as Mummy's assistant, and by "volunteered," I mean I followed her around the kitchen, *helping* with every step of the food preparation. My job? Taste-testing, of course.

Now let me tell you about the spread—canapés so delicate they looked like art, sandwiches bursting with flavour, and Mama's absolute favourite: a luscious tiramisu. There were also cookies, cakes, and so many delicious treats it felt like a buffet of dreams. My contributions to the process? Legendary. I bravely cleaned up every crumb that dared to hit the floor, ensuring the kitchen stayed spotless. There was a particularly daring moment when a canapé *almost* escaped into the wild—I intercepted it mid-roll, saving the day. My work here was heroic, if I do say so myself.

When Mama finally came downstairs, I could hardly contain my excitement. She had no idea what we'd planned! After giving her our gifts—which she absolutely adored, especially mine—I basked in her cuddles and kisses. I could see the gears turning in her head; she knew we were up to something, but she didn't know just how fabulous the day was about to get.

Then it happened. The buzzer rang. It was midday, and the moment of truth had arrived. Mummy told Mama to answer the door, and when she opened it, there stood her brothers and sisters— Uncle David, Uncle Rod, Aunty Jane, and Aunty Ali. Mama's face lit up with pure joy. Me? I lost all self-control.

I launched myself into action, charging across the room at top speed. My paws skidded on the floor like I was auditioning for a puggy ice-skating team. *THUD* into the wall. But did that stop me? Absolutely not. I leapt up, tail wagging furiously, and showered the guests with my exuberant puggy love. Did I maybe overstay my welcome? Perhaps. Let's just say Uncle David probably didn't *ask* for a lap full of enthusiastic pug.

Oh, Uncle David's lap was my throne, but then came Uncle Rod, my new partner in crime! Uncle Rod was a hoot. He'd cheer me on, "Go on, Phil! Jump higher!" And boy, did I jump! I bounced around the sofa like a little pogo stick, my tail wagging like a propeller. Uncle Rod would laugh and clap, and I'd get even more excited. I'd leap onto the cushions, do a little spin, and then pounce on my squeaky toy. Uncle Rod was my biggest fan, and together, we turned the living room into our playground. It was pure puggy pandemonium!

To restore order, Mama tried to calm me down by putting me in another room with the cats. *The cats!* I mean, really? They greeted me with their usual disdain—Saffron glaring like I'd disrupted her 14th nap of the day, and Zachary pretending I didn't exist. Needless to say, I was thrilled when my family eventually let me back into the party… on the condition that I behaved.

I settled onto the sofa with Mama and Mummy, trying my best to stay cool despite the room feeling like a furnace. The party was in full swing—laughter, stories, and most importantly, food. The guests marvelled at the spread (rightfully so, since I was basically the sous chef), and when the tiramisu made its grand entrance? Oh, the applause! Mama was over the moon, and I, of course, took full credit for its success.

As the party wound down, I curled up next to my Mummies, feeling proud of the day's triumphs. I'd been the selfless cleaner, the fearless greeter, and the life of the party. Mama's birthday was a smashing success, and even though I wasn't the star (for once), I was perfectly content. After all, what's a party without a little puggy magic?

🐾 Chapter 19: Phil's Social Media Takeover: The Rise of a Pug Legend

Once, I was a humble pup—a creature of comfort, mischief, and snack-fuelled adventures. My world consisted of zoomies, belly rubs, and the occasional strategic battle against the injustice of denied hooman food. But then… *everything changed.*

Through the magic of Instagram, my face—*this regal pug mug*—graced the timelines of hoomans and fellow doggos worldwide. One post. Then another. Then chaos. My charm was undeniable. My expressions? Iconic. My antics? Legendary. Slowly, the numbers grew—from a handful of admirers to thousands, then a pug-powered empire of loyal followers.

But then came… TikTok.

And suddenly, my chaos was not just seen—it was *felt.* It was *heard.* It was *celebrated!*

🐾 The puppy days? Adorable. 🐾 The first stairs video? Legendary. 🐾 The begging face? *Unmatched.*

I started with innocent, humble posts—a cute pose here, a belly rub moment there, just a little glimpse into my daily puggy excellence. Then, the world caught on. The followers grew. The comments rolled in. The engagement skyrocketed.

I built an inner circle—a squad of fellow pups: Harry, Mylo, Idah-Rose, Murphy, Sammy, Dave, Rigby, Sir Jeeves, Frankie, Barry, and my love pug, Duckie, fans, and dedicated hoomans who celebrated my milestones, tagged me in memes, and appreciated my undeniable greatness.

Instagram was mine. My domain. My kingdom of chaos and cuteness. And then I thought, why stop at photos? Why limit myself to still images when my true mischief needed movement?

It was time for **TikTok**.

🐾 A head tilt? Viral. 🐾 A dramatic zoomie moment? Instant engagement. 🐾 My war against pigeons? The world *needed* to see it.

TikTok was where my true chaos could thrive—where my zoomies could be celebrated in cinematic perfection, and my sass could be viewed in real-time.

The likes began pouring in—from hundreds to *thousands* to well over 12,000! I had officially become a social media legend. Make **no** mistake—this isn't just about numbers.

This is about connection.

This is about sharing my greatest moments—my dramatic pigeon conquests, my snack-related tragedies, my relentless battles against doggos who ignore my existence. Through Instagram and TikTok, my kingdom expanded, reaching hoomans far and wide, ensuring that everyone—EVERYONE—knew the pug named *PHIL*. And so, I continue my reign—posting, engaging, delivering chaos, sass, and pug wisdom to the masses.

For *I am Phil. The Pug Icon. The Social Media Star. The Undisputed King of Engagement.*

And this empire is only growing.

🐾 Chapter 20: The Sleep Saga: Phil vs. The Inevitable Nap

Ah, sleep—the age-old battle between exhaustion and my unbreakable determination to stay awake. But while most pugs surrender to slumber anywhere, I, Phil the Pug, have carefully curated my elite napping spots for maximum comfort and drama.

You see, I have **FOMO**—Fear of Missing Out. If something is happening, if there is excitement in the air, you best believe I am staying awake to witness every second. Sleep is for later! Fun is *now!* And so, in my valiant efforts, I have mastered the art of fighting off slumber until my body quite literally shuts down against my will.

There have been times when, mid-fetch, mid-tug-of-war, mid-*life itself,* I simply… *dropped.* Gone. Eyes closed, paws sprawled, right in the middle of the action. One second, I'm chasing glory, the next I'm unconscious on the battlefield. My humans have learned to recognize the signs. The droopy eyelids. The swaying stance. The subtle head bob that means *oh no, it's happening again.*

And then there are my sacred sleep spots.

Let's start with my **daytime throne**: the *back of the sofa*. A true pug king doesn't nap like a commoner; no, he ascends. With a mighty leap onto the cushions, I clamber up to my lofty perch, gazing upon my kingdom like a watchful ruler… and then promptly curl into a cozy ball of sleepy bliss.

However, there exists a hidden trick in my puggy playbook. If no hooman is present to witness my glorious ascent, I deploy *The Stuck Act™*. With expert timing, I let out a heart-wrenching cry for help, convincing my humans that I am trapped in a perilous predicament. They rush in, filled with concern, ready to rescue me. But the moment they reach out? I miraculously free myself, casually strolling away as if nothing happened.

You see, in the art of being a pug, the drama is just as important as the nap. And I? I am an Oscar-worthy performer.

During the day, the bed is my kingdom. I sink into its embrace, curling up in blankets with the determination of a creature who has *earned* that nap. Early mornings? Absolutely not. While the world wakes up, I remain under the duvet, a glorious loaf of resistance.

And yet, no matter where my daytime naps take me, *nighttime* remains the pinnacle of my ritual.

Ah yes, the *kneading* begins.

I grip my beloved donut, pressing and squeezing in rhythmic movements. My breathing grows heavier, my shoulders shift. My Mummies watch in fascination, wondering what mysterious ancient pug ritual this is.

The answer is simple: Ultimate relaxation. And then—*I am gone.* Eyes closed, body limp, dreams of belly rub victories, and protecting my Manor swirling in my mind.

Night falls. The house is quiet. The humans believe they have won. *Fools!* They have removed me from my rightful throne, forcing me onto the mattress below. But I? I am relentless.

As soon as Mama lays her head on the pillow, the moment arrives—the sign, the invitation. I leap, claiming my rightful place upon her pillow, snuggling into the very spot meant for her head. And there I remain.

Snoring. Dreaming. Untouchable. Until, of course, reality strikes—her head has no room, she tries to shift, and I am relocated. But I? I *always* return. Like a knight reclaiming his throne, I wiggle back to my rightful pillow position.

Like a shadow in the darkness, I plot my revenge. I wait until their defences are weak, until their eyes grow heavy with sleep. And then... I strike!

With stealth unmatched, I wiggle, shimmy, and climb, slowly reclaiming my pillow kingdom. I curl into place, victorious. My Mama stirs, realizing the deception. *Too late.* I am already snoring.

Once removed, I always return. It is destiny. And so, this cycle continues, night after night, battle after battle. Sleep always wins in the end, but I? I make it *fight for victory.*

If sleep were a competitive sport, I would be the undefeated champion.

🥇 **Gold Medal in Sleep-Standing™:** Yes, I have fallen asleep while standing. My Mummies have witnessed it, confused yet impressed. I swayed. I blinked. And then? *Gone.*

🥈 **Silver Medal in Mid-Tug-Nap™:** Few pugs can say they have fallen asleep while playing. One moment I am gripping my toy with determination, the next… my paws release and I am down, snoring before the toy even hits the ground.

🥉 **Bronze Medal in Pillow Theft™:** Sleeping **on** Mama's pillow is not just a habit—it's a sport. My ability to reclaim the exact same spot, even after multiple relocations, is unparalleled athleticism.

I am Phil the Sleep Pug Olympian, a legend in the world of competitive snoozing. No pug has ever done it better.

Morning arrives. My Mummies wake up, stretch, make strange groggy noises—but I? I refuse.

The duvet is my fortress, my sanctuary, my safe haven against the cruelty of early mornings. My Mummies try everything to extract me— sweet voices, gentle encouragement, even lifting the duvet like an eviction notice. I pretend not to hear, burying myself deeper, embracing the soft fabric like it's my final lifeline.

But then… the smell hits me. Breakfast. *Already waiting.*

My tail betrays me, wagging against my will. My eyes open slightly. My resolve weakens. Then, in a dramatic display of resilience, I rise— stretching, sighing heavily, making sure everyone understands that this is against my wishes.

I march toward my grand feast, still half-asleep but determined. The food vanishes instantly (I don't know how; my Mummies claim I inhale it), and in a moment of pure pug gratitude, I bestow kisses upon my mummies—a thank-you for their service.

🐾 Chapter 21: The Pug Toy Olympics: Tug, Fetch, and Ultimate Destruction™

The feast has replenished my energy, and battle begins.

My trusted weapons—Penguin plush and sacred donut toy—are presented. The hoomans dare to challenge me in tug-of-war, unaware that I am the undefeated champion. With pure determination, I grip, pull, shake—sometimes I growl dramatically to increase the tension.

Then comes fetch—where I chase the toy like a warrior, grab it… and immediately refuse to return it. What is life without a little suspense?

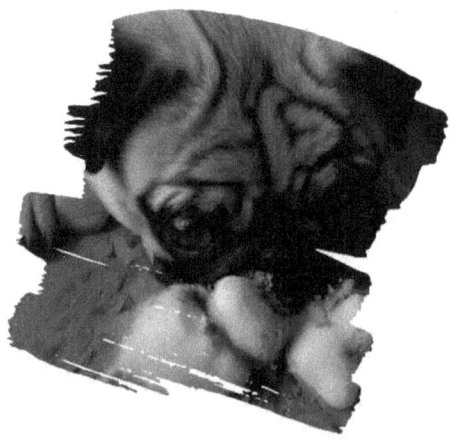

Of course, some toys perish in battle. The shredded remains lay before me—evidence of my victory, a reminder that I am a true conqueror. My Mummies, however, often say things like *"Phil, that was brand new"*—a statement irrelevant to my puggy pursuits.

My Mummies may not appreciate the smell of my toys, but to me? Pure bliss. A symphony of chewed plush, slobber, and mystery Odors that only a true pug can understand.

With energy still flowing, it's time for martial arts training.

I **r**oll onto my back, legs kicking wildly as if preparing for a showdown in an action movie. My Mummies approach, offering belly rubs. A rookie mistake!

I attempt gentle combat, swiping at their hand, playfully biting (not hard, because I love them, obviously). My Mummies laugh, thinking it's playtime, but I'm honing my pug warrior skills.

The answer is simple: Ultimate relaxation. And then—*I am gone.* Eyes closed, body limp, dreams of belly rub victories, and protecting my Manor swirling in my mind!

🐾 Chapter 22: Leg-Zigzags, Jogger Crimes & Pigeon Disappointments: The Walkies Chronicles

It begins with excitement overload.

I SEE THE SIGNS.

My Mummies are gathering their belongings. The whispers of "walkies" start to swirl through the air. And then…

THE HARNESS APPEARS.

Oh. Oh, this is happening.

THIS IS IT. THE MOMENT HAS ARRIVED.

Like a pug possessed, I bounce, I twist, I attempt to grab my harness straight from Mama or Mummy's hands. I must seize it. Claim it. Control my destiny. But NO! They refuse to let me take command of my own fate. They say I must calm down.

CALM? RIDICULOUS.

I zigzag between legs, weaving through their steps like a four-legged hurricane, my tiny body an unstoppable force—a challenge that my Mummies *never* seem prepared for. They trip. They stumble. They utter noises of exasperation. *I am winning.*

BUT THEN… THE SHOES.

Ah, the fatal error of hoomans everywhere. Their feet are vulnerable. Their shoes are unguarded. This is an open invitation for battle— **FOOT & SHOE WAR™** *HAS BEGUN!* I pounce. I nip at toes. I attempt to wrestle a shoe into submission. Because clearly, shoes are not necessary when walkies are at stake.

And yet…they win! The shoes are securely fastened, the harness finally locked into place and now comes the leash. I AM TOO READY. I run to the door. I run back to push them forward. I run to the door again. I run back for another encouraging leg jump. They say, "Wait." I ignore. They say, "Wait, Phil." I consider. They say, "Just STOP for one second." I pause dramatically.

The leash battle begins! I do my best tug-of-war to stop this bad boy from being attached – but my Mummies always and win and it's eventually fastened. The door opens. I emerge like a royal guardian stepping into his domain.

Will today's walk be a neighbourhood prowl, where I reclaim territory and deposit Phil Juice on outrageously marked locations? Or shall we visit Phil's Manor Park, my sacred land, my place of freedom and prestige?

As a pug of great stature, it is my duty to reclaim my territory from unworthy trespassers. I inspect every spot; lamppost, corner, brick wall, fence, post-box sniffing for clues of intruding doggos who have dared mark my land. I respond accordingly with a warning, a reclaim and a message of dominance

PHIL JUICE HAS BEEN DEPLOYED.

The kingdom is secure.

Ah, but the journey is never without unexpected encounters in Phil's Manor Park—the land of freedom, zoomies, and unpredictable doggo diplomacy. There are many types of doggos here:

🐾 **THE WORTHY WARRIORS**—those who engage in the sacred zoomie battles. We circle, dash, tumble—a fleeting moment of mutual canine greatness.

🐾 **THE RUDE REJECTORS**—those who take one look at me and run away!

Excuse me?! I am adorable. I am majestic. I am fun. Why do they reject me?! I stand there, betrayed, watching their retreat in puggy disbelief. I shake my head and run back to my Mummies sad and hurt. Unforgivable.

And then, we encounter the true villains.

Oh, the joggers.

The relentless invaders of my tranquil Manor. They appear from nowhere, disturbing my patrol, running in endless loops with no destination, no clear purpose. WHY? What are they chasing?

DO THEY EVER CATCH IT?!

At first, I observe them with confusion. Then, I attempt engagement—a bark, a chase, an invitation to interact. NOTHING. They do not acknowledge my existence. They simply…KEEP RUNNING. I watch them vanish into the distance, still pondering their mission. I may never know.

95

Then there's the pigeons – the deceivers!

The greatest deceivers of all time. They land near me, bobbing their heads, pretending to be friendly, approachable, interactive. And then—

I make my move. A sprint. A charge. The ultimate moment of engagement! And just when I think—*finally*, some action! — they leave. WHY?! Why do they exist if their entire purpose is sitting, waiting, and fleeing?! Do they have hobbies? *Ambitions?* A greater purpose in life?

NO. Just bobbling heads and bad decisions!

And then, there are the lake dwellers.

"Oh, look at me, I can float," says the duck. "I am elegant and untouchable," says the swan.

BIG DEAL.

What do they even DO?! Just exist on water? Make weird noises? They don't run. They don't forage. They don't experience the thrill of chasing squirrels.

Truly, what a wasted life.

And so, with another successful day of patrol, play, and evaluating useless birds, I return home. I have protected the kingdom, judged the birds, and survived the jogger invasion!

Victorious. Accomplished and ready for my next extraordinary nap!

For I am Phil—Pug King, Supreme Judge of Birdkind, and Reluctant Morning Warrior.

🐾 Chapter 23: Denied, Deprived, But Never Defeated: A Pug's Battle for Snacks

Ah, the hooman feast. A spectacle, a betrayal, a moment of great injustice. Roast dinners, pizza, chicken, omelettes, eggs, steak, all within reach, yet somehow off-limits. I am Phil, the Master of Silent Protest. I do not whine. I do not bark. No—I use the eyes.

The puppy eyes technique is a craft, an art perfected over time. First, I lower my head gently, resting my chin on Mama or Mummy's arm or leg, peering up at the plate.

Then, the look of pure heartbreak emerges—eyes wide, hopeful, filled with a sorrow no hooman could possibly ignore. And yet—they ignore it. They laugh. They dismiss my suffering. They say "No, Phil, this is not for you."

A lie. Food is *always* for me.

And so, defeated yet determined, I return to my backup plan: watching their every movement with deep intensity, ensuring that at any moment, an opportunity may arise. Occasionally this does worky my Puggy friends!

But let me tell you about the things I *am* allowed – starting with Pup Cups – every Puggy and doggos dream treat!

The fluffy, creamy delight that brings joy beyond words. My Mummies present it like a sacred offering, and suddenly—everything changes. The world becomes brighter, time slows, my tail transforms into a blur of excitement.

I lock onto my prize. Foam, delicious, silky foam. My tongue moves faster than thought, scooping, slurping, devouring. I am in a state of pure ecstasy. Then, the cup is empty.

I pause. I stare. I scan the environment, desperate for more. But alas— the hoomans are cruel. There is no second round. I throw one last hopeful glance toward my mummies. They laugh, pat my head, say "All gone, Phil."

Tragic.

Which brings me onto my prized possessions—the Yakers Yak chews, chicken calcium bones, chew sticks—each one a masterpiece of pure delight. Some must be devoured immediately, claimed as my rightful prize. But others? Others must be preserved.

The chew stick ritual is one of great precision.

Phase One: The Devouring. The chicken is strategically stripped away, enjoyed with careful bites, ensuring maximum flavour extraction.

Phase Two: The Preservation. The remaining chew is hidden, placed in a **secret location**, a place only I shall know.

Phase Three: The Daily Return. Each day, I revisit my treasure, gnawing with controlled intensity, savouring my victory bit by bit.

Phase Four: The Re-Hiding. After an appropriate chew session, the stick must be hidden once more, because one must never consume all their riches in a single sitting.

I am Phil, the Pug of Preservation, the Guardian of Hidden Snacks, the Strategic Food Hoarder.

Chapter 24: Phil and the Culinary Event of a Lifetime: The Pizza Spectacle

Ah, pizza night—the most anticipated event in my universe. The moment my Mummy rolls up her sleeves, dusts the kitchen table with flour, and begins the sacred dough ritual, I know.

I perch upon the sofa, positioned perfectly to witness every movement. From the first knead to the final toppings, I observe, I analyse, I prepare. My eyes never leave her hands—because I, *Phil*, understand that we are on the brink of greatness.

The flour is spread. The dough is formed. The kneading begins, a bit like when I knead my favourite toys!

Ah, yes—the rhythmic pressing, stretching, rolling. It is a dance of artistry, a performance so hypnotizing that I must watch in absolute silence. With each roll of the pin, my excitement grows. Every sprinkle of flour, every twist of the dough—it all builds toward the moment of truth.

Of course, I am a team player. If flour has fallen to the floor, I step in to help. *No need to grab a cloth, Mummy—I've got this.* With great dedication, I lick the mess away, ensuring that the kitchen remains spotless. I am efficient, thorough, and deeply committed to my work.

But I must be quick as then comes the toppings—the grand transformation. I do not want to miss that!

Cheese, sauce, meats, vegetables—each ingredient placed with precision and purpose. The moment the cheese is sprinkled, I begin wiggling uncontrollably. This is not just food. *This is art.*

But then—oh, glorious day—*MY* pizza appears.

A Phil-sized masterpiece, crafted just for me. A perfect circle of joy. My tail becomes a blur. I let out whimpers of pure excitement. I watch every single movement, as if ensuring quality control.

Into the oven it goes. This is where things get intense. I position myself closer to the oven. I stare inside, watching as the magic unfolds. The cheese begins to bubble, the crust grows golden, and I lose all sense of time and space.

Occasionally, I turn to my Mummy with a look of impatience. *Is it ready now? What about now? How about now?*

She says, "Not yet, Phil."

Finally, the oven door is opened, the luxury smell of MY pizza makes my Puggy brain go into overdrive! And I lose my mind. The pizza emerges from the fiery depths, glorious, perfect, the greatest achievement of all time.

I bounce. I twist. I celebrate. My Mummy giggles, but they do not understand the gravity of this moment. The pizza is placed before me. I inhale deeply, savouring the aroma of victory.

And then—I devour.

For I am Phil, the Supreme Pizza Enthusiast, the Guardian of Dough, the Cleanup Crew Extraordinaire.

🐾 Chapter 25: Puggies of the Carribean: The Legendary Birthday of Captain Phil!

Ahoy, me hearties! Gather 'round, for I am about to recount the most **epic** birthday adventure in pug history. The day I turned *one whole year old*—a day of triumph, terror (mostly thanks to rogue balloons), and **treasure beyond imagination!**

The morning began with an air of mystery. I sensed something was different. The lounge had transformed into a pirate's paradise—banners with *my name*, puggy decorations hanging from the ceiling, and most thrilling of all... two treasure chests overflowing with presents! I was the captain, the ruler of the high seas, the fiercest *puganeer* to ever sail the sofa cushions.

I donned my custom-made pirate costume, feeling every bit the adventurous legend. The crew assembled, my loyal Instagram mates— 3,000 followers strong—dressed up in their finest pirate attire and tagged me in their posts, honouring the great Captain Phil. The celebration had begun!

But then—*tragedy struck!*

Three monstrous helium pug balloons loomed before me, towering, watching... and CHASING. Every time I moved, they followed! I barked, I ran, I darted under tables—why were these sky beasts after me?! Were they pirate ghosts? Haunted spirits of the Puggy Seas?! I made a daring escape, but they haunted my dreams for days.

But the day had a tragedy—Mama had to depart for work, leaving me in the capable hands of Mummy.

106

Was I devastated? Yes. Was I dramatic? Absolutely. But did I turn this betrayal into an EPIC ADVENTURE? You bet your biscuit-loving paws I did!

For today, Mummy and I embarked on the journey of legends—a cinematic feast known as…

🏴‍☠️ **Pirates of the Caribbean.** 🏴‍☠️

From the very first scene, I KNEW.

The chaos, the mischief, the absolute refusal to follow the rules—I saw myself reflected in every single movement of Captain Jack Sparrow. The swagger. The witty comebacks. The ability to turn disaster into triumph with sheer charm and ridiculous confidence.

THIS WAS ME. THIS WAS MY SPIRIT.

I studied his movements carefully, occasionally tilting my head in deep puggy analysis. And then, it hit me. I was not just watching *Captain Jack Sparrow.* I *was* Captain Phil Sparrow.

The Unpredictable Walking Style—Jack Sparrow's chaotic, zigzagging movements? Oh, please. That's just how I approach doorways, food bowls, and any sudden excitement!

The Unstoppable Confidence—Jack Sparrow NEVER stops, NEVER doubts himself, and ALWAYS acts like he's in control—even when things are falling apart.

Oh? Sounds familiar? That's me attempting to steal a shoe before a walkies session.

The Swaggy Dramatic Pauses—Oh, Jack, you think you invented the dramatic pause? That's adorable.

I, Phil, pause dramatically every time I hear the fridge open, every time Mummy tells me to "wait" before walkies, and every single time a snack is placed before me just out of reach.

The Unwavering Dedication to Treasure (A.K.A Snacks)—Jack will risk everything for gold, trinkets, and mystical treasures.

I will risk EVERYTHING to obtain hooman food.

By the end of the movie, there was no denying it—I had become the legendary pug pirate of my time. I stared into the distance, contemplating my next mischievous conquest.

I needed a pirate hat. I needed a ship. But most of all… I needed snacks.

For I am Captain Phil Sparrow—The Rogue Pug of the Caribbean, The Supreme Snack Thief, The Untamed Adventurer of Pillow and Blanket Realms.

When Mama finally returned, oh, how we celebrated in full force! Then came the **feast**. Mummy had crafted a masterpiece—a cake fit for a pug king. Special party treats were laid out for all. I stuffed my little face with glee, knowing that no pirate ever sails on an empty stomach! The grand feast, the cuddles, the joyous reunions—it was glorious.

As the festivities wound down, I curled up atop my treasure, victorious. The legend of *Puggies of the Caribbean* had been written, and **Captain Phil had conquered his first year in style!**

And so, my loyal crew, remember this day well—for it shall go down in history as the greatest pug birthday adventure of all time!

🐾 Chapter 26: The Beginning of My Puggy Legacy

Ahem.

Well, hoomans, we've reached the end of this book—but let's get one thing straight: this is *NOT* the end of my story.

No, no, no.

If anything, this is merely the beginning.

Let's take a moment to reflect on my first year, shall we?

I arrived—a tiny, wrinkly pug with big ambitions and an even bigger personality. I didn't just enter this world. I claimed it. I conquered the household. Every blanket? Mine. Every lap? Mine. Every sofa? Decidedly, unapologetically mine.

I embarked on snack-related quests. Some successful (*The Pizza Spectacle remains one of my finest moments*), some tragically thwarted (*The Great Deprivation of Treats will forever haunt me*). I earned my title as King of Cuteness and Comfort.

I mastered the art of zoomies, embraced the luxury of bath-time spa days, and perfected the puggy pout that bends hoomans to my will.

I sought feline friendships. A noble effort—met with rejection, indifference, and the occasional judgmental stare. This battle remains ongoing, and I'm certain lots more to come!

I celebrated, explored, and made every day an adventure. Be it birthdays, holidays, or surprise parties—I made sure to be at the centre of it all.

But more than all of that—this year has been about something greater.

It's been about **love.**

There are more snacks to earn. More zoomies to run. More feline & doggo friendships (or battles) to pursue. More adventures waiting just beyond my paws.

Stay tuned for the *next chapter* in Phil's story—the journey of a pug who isn't just ruling his household but **pugging the world!**

🐾 Bonus Section: Puggy Perks & Mischief!

🐾 The Official Pug Commandments

As King of Cuteness and Comfort, I have rules—strict laws for my hooman servants to follow. Ignoring these? A serious offense.

🐾 Thou shalt never deny snacks. Snack time is sacred. If I want food, I *must* receive food.

🐾 Zoomies must be respected at *all* times. If I suddenly launch into an Olympic-level sprint around the house? Let me be. I am working on my speed.

🐾 All furniture belongs to Phil—no exceptions. If you sit on my sofa, it is by my permission only and expect to be celebrated with Pug Glitter all over your clothes!

🐾 Baths are good, but drying MUST involve zoomies. A freshly cleaned pug requires maximum speed and chaos post-bath.

💡 Phil's Ultimate Life Tips

Want to live like a pug legend? Take notes, hoomans.

"If you stare long enough, the snacks will come to you."

"There is no such thing as too many naps—only too few blankets."

"Confidence, determination, and extreme cuteness are the keys to success."

🌍 Pugging the World: Phil's Social Crew!

I may rule my household, but I also have an empire of online friends—pugs, Boston Terriers, cats, and hoomans who have joined my reign!

🐾 **Mylo Murphy**—The boss, the CEO, my fearless leader from Galway, Ireland.

🐾 **Harry the Boston Terrier**—My cute bestie from Dublin and loyal friend since Scrappy's days.

🐾 **Murphy the British Blue Cat**—Looks like Zachary but is devoted to me (an actual miracle).

🐾 **Idah-Rose**—Champagne-loving pug royalty, Mylo's girlfriend, a true queen.

🐾 **Dave Puggo**—My long-lost pug twin from Scotland—our resemblance is uncanny.

🐾 **Sammy from the USA**—A legend, a fellow Mylo & Mas employee, a true friend.

🐾 **Barry the Black Pug**—A comedic genius and video entertainer extraordinaire.

🐾 **Duckie from Canada**—My **love pug**, my sweetheart across the seas.

🐾 **Teddy from Devon**—My pawmazing bestie, so loyal and caring. The cutest Pug in the South West.

🐾 **Sir Jeeves**—The tartan extraordinaire who I admire, respect and look up to.

🐾 **Mousey the Chi**—Stylish London Chihuahua with the coolest parents and formidable style.

🐾 Phil's Top Expressions & Puggy Poses

🐾 **The "Snack Stare"**—A deeply persuasive technique. Stare at hoomans until they break and hand over food.

🐾 **The "Judgmental Side-Eye"**—Reserved for moments of deep betrayal, such as snack denial or being ignored by cats.

🐾 **The "Blanket Burrito"**—The perfect nap formation. Maximum comfort. Maximum coziness.

🐾 Puggy Mad Libs – Create Your Own Phil Story!

Here's your chance to write a pug-powered adventure! Fill in the blanks below to make *your* own ridiculous Phil tale:

"One day, Phil woke up and decided to _____ (verb). He put on his _____ (adjective) crown and set off on a mission to find _____ (noun). Along the way, he encountered _____ (funny animal), who tried to steal his _____ (snack). But Phil, being the master of _____ (pug skill), managed to escape with _____ (victory moment). And so, another day of puggy greatness was complete!"

📖 Fan Club Call to Action!

Want more Phil adventures, snack heists, and feline friendship attempts? Follow me online!

📷 **Instagram** @phil_the_pug_star

📷 **TikTok:** *@philthepug*

📧 **e-mail:** *PhilThePug@outlook.com*

Join the *pug-powered movement*!

About the Author(s) Phil the Pug— Lord of the Manor, Snack Warrior, Ruler of All Things Cozy

Ahem.

Let's be clear about something. *I am not just any pug.*

I am **Phil.**

Lord of the Manor. Defender of the Kingdom. Master of Snacks. Protector of Hoomans. Sworn Enemy of Joggers. Reluctant Observer of Boring Ducks.

Since the moment I arrived, I have dedicated my life to greatness.

It is my duty to patrol the Manor grounds, ensuring no unauthorized joggers' trespass on my territory. It is my responsibility to glare at the ducks (who are dull and contribute nothing to society). It is my mission to outsmart my hoomans and retrieve snacks at all costs.

In my first year alone, I have: Claimed every cushion, sofa, and blanket as my rightful throne. Established dominance over all things soft and cozy. Created an intricate defence strategy to keep joggers at bay. Initiated several peace talks with the household cats (all unsuccessful). Engineered multiple snack-related heists with varying degrees of success. Conquered Mount Staircase. Damaged my right eye to almost destruction, but I fought back and fully recovered!

But this book? *It isn't just about my victories.*

It is about legacy.

But I did not tell this story alone, I had *Mama*.

📖 Phil's Mama—The Storyteller Behind the Pugginess

Every great tale needs a narrator, someone who captures the madness, the triumphs, the zoomies, and the snack-related scandals in a way that does them justice.

That's where Phil's Mama, Kaz Rance, comes in.

With Phil, it was love at first sight when they met for the very first time. She had no idea what an impact he would have on her or her partner, Tina. He stole their hearts instantly.

She has been there for every milestone, every adventure, every dramatic showdown between Phil and the household cats. She is the keeper of memories, the one who ensures that Phil's greatness is properly documented—from his grand Manor patrols to his ongoing battle against joggers (*who, frankly, are far too energetic*), the cats, and his forever quest for food!

This is Kaz's first book, and is the start of a series of Puggy Tales from Phil. His love, determination and loyalty has inspired her creative mind to get to work.

And with Phil's reign far from over expect more fun and exciting stories from this duo!

🐾 Glossary Puggy Terms

Zoomies

(noun) /ˈzuː.miːz/ **Definition:** The sudden, uncontrollable urge to sprint at maximum speed in random directions, usually after a bath or before bedtime. **Not optional. Example:** *"Stand back—Phil's got the zoomies!"*

Phil Juice

(noun) /ˈfɪl dʒuːs/ **Definition:** The mysterious, exclusive beverage exchanged between Phil and Idah-Rose. Contents remain **classified. Example:** *"One bottle of Phil Juice coming right up!"*

Jogger Crimes

(noun) /ˈdʒɒg.ər kraɪmz/ **Definition:** The **deeply offensive** act of hoomans running through **Phil's Manor territory** without his permission. Punishable by excessive puggy side-eye. **Example:** *"Alert! Joggers detected—activate Phil patrol!"*

Blanket Burrito

(noun) /ˈblæŋ.kɪt bəˈriː.toʊ/ **Definition:** The **optimal sleep formation** for maximum coziness. Requires **full blanket wrap, head peeking out slightly, and zero disturbances. Example:** *"Phil has achieved Blanket Burrito mode—no hooman shall wake him now."*

Boring Ducks

(noun) /ˈbɔː.rɪŋ dʌks/ **Definition:** Waterfowl that Phil has **deemed uninteresting. Example:** *"Why do they just sit there doing nothing? What's the point?!"*

Feline Betrayal

(noun) /ˈfiː.laɪn bɪˈtreɪ.əl/ **Definition:** The **refusal of household cats to acknowledge Phil's greatness** or accept his offers of friendship. **Example:** *"Phil tried the puppy eyes again. The cats ignored him. Another day of feline betrayal."*

Puglic Pee-fection Moment

(noun) /ˈpʌg.lɪk piːˈfɛk.ʃən/ **Definition:** The **dramatic, ceremonial act** of Phil finding **the perfect spot** to relieve himself—often requiring multiple laps and deep contemplation. **Example:** *"This patch of grass does not meet my standards—onward!"*

Snack Negotiation Stare

(noun) /snæk nəˌgoʊ.ʃiˈeɪ.ʃən stɛr/ **Definition:** The **highly skilled tactic** of staring at hoomans **until snacks are surrendered. Example:** *"You will hand over the treats. It is inevitable."*

Paw-litical Drama

(noun) /pɔː.lɪ.tɪ.kəl ˈdrɑː.mə/ **Definition:** Any situation in which **Phil's leadership is questioned, snacks are unfairly withheld, or feline alliances disrupt his reign. Example:** *"Today, I was refused a second breakfast. The paw-litical fallout will be severe."*

Pug Royalty Protocol

(noun) /pʌg rɔɪˈæl.ti prəʊ.tə.kɒl/ **Definition:** The strict rules hoomans must follow when dealing with **His Royal Pugness** (Phil). Includes **proper food offerings, belly rub tributes, and the respectful surrender of all furniture. Example:** *"Excuse me, hooman, you seem to be sitting on MY throne (the sofa). Immediate relocation is required."*

The Great Staircase Conquest

(noun) /ðə greɪt ˈstɛə.keɪs ˈkɒn.kwɛst/ **Definition:** The **legendary battle** Phil faced while **attempting to master stairs**, a struggle filled with *determination, wobbly climbs, and eventual triumphant victory.* **Example:** *"Today, I climbed the stairs. Tomorrow, I conquer the world."*

Snackless Injustice

(noun) /snæk.ləs ɪnˈdʒʌs.tɪs/ **Definition:** The **truly devastating** moment when Phil is **denied food**, whether by poor hooman decisions or catastrophic snack shortages. **Example:** *"The hooman ate all the pizza and gave me NOTHING. I have suffered Snackless Injustice today."*

The Pug Toy-Olympics

(noun) /pʌg tɔɪ ɒlˈɪm.pɪks/ **Definition:** The **high-energy sporting event** in which Phil tests the **durability, chew resistance, and throwability** of his many toys. Typically ends with **total destruction of all** participants. **Example:** *"In today's Pug Toy-Olympics, Phil obliterated three stuffed animals, a rubber bone, and a squeaky duck. Gold medal performance."*

Midnight Snack Patrol

(noun) /ˈmɪd.naɪt snæk pəˈtrəʊl/ **Definition:** The **stealthy, tactical reconnaissance mission** Phil embarks upon at night, scouring the floor for **crumbs, abandoned treats, or suspicious snack opportunities. Example:** *"Phil is on Midnight Snack Patrol. The kitchen must be thoroughly inspected for unguarded morsels."*

The Puggy Resistance

(noun) /pʌg.i rɪˈzɪs.təns/ **Definition:** Phil's **staunch rebellion against bath time, vet visits, or any unwanted hooman interference with his freedom. Example:** *"The mummies tried to put me in a harness. The Puggy Resistance was activated immediately."*

Pigeon Disappointment

(noun) /ˈpɪdʒ.ən dɪs.əˈpɔɪnt.mənt/ **Definition:** The moment of **deep frustration** when Phil sees a pigeon, approaches with *intense curiosity*, and realizes **it is not fun at all. Example:** *"Phil spotted a pigeon and prepared for greatness. It did nothing. Pigeon Disappointment was experienced."*

🐾 Acknowledgements

🐾 From Phil – The Pug Who Would Like to Express His Greatness & Gratitude

Ahem.

Before I wrap up this glorious, snack-filled literary masterpiece, I must take a moment to thank the key figures in my legendary life—those who have supported my reign, tolerated my zoomies, and witnessed the full power of Phil-ness.

🏠 **To my Mummy Tina, Mama Kaz, and Hooman Sister Ezra—** What can I say? You are my forever family. You are my home, my world, my snack suppliers, my belly rub specialists. Without you, I would not have the Manor to protect, the joggers to glare at, or the boring ducks to avoid. You make my life perfect, and for that, I will never stop snuggling you or strategically sitting on your laps until you give me extra treats.

🐶 **To Froggo & Pumpkin**, my birth parents—Thank you for blessing me with maximum cuteness, prime snacking abilities, and an undeniable talent for ruling hoomans with sheer adorableness. You gave me the gift of pug greatness, and I intend to use it wisely (for snacks).

🐾 **To my Nanny, Hannah**—For caring for me in my tiniest, wobbliest puppy days. You were my first protector, my first cuddle provider, and my first witness to my snack-stealing talents.

🐱 **To Zachary and Saffron**—My feline housemates, my reluctant companions, my long-standing sources of rejection. Even though you mostly ignore me, I acknowledge your existence. And should you ever decide to befriend me, I will not hold a grudge (probably).

🐾 **To Mylo & Mas Boutique**—For recognizing my undeniable star power and welcoming me as their **official Brand Rep.** Thank you for providing me with an elite harness collection that makes me look stylish, powerful, and ready to conquer the world one strut at a time. **Mylo, Martina, and Michaela**—You are a formidable trio who keep Mylo & Mas running with excellence, charm, and a keen eye for top-tier pug fashion. You have outfitted me with greatness, and for that, I promise to wear my harnesses with pride, confidence, and just the right amount of sass.

📸 **To my legendary Instagram crew**—Mylo Murphy, Harry, Murphy the Cat, Idah-Rose, Dave Puggo, Sammy, Barry, Tofu, Teddy, Frankie, Mase, James, Mousey, Sir Jeeves, and my love, Duckie – in fact *all my followers!* You are my global puggy empire, my loyal crew, my fellow snack warriors. Without you, this book would not exist. Without you, I would not be Phil, Pug of the People.

Now, if everyone will excuse me, I must conclude these acknowledgments before snack time expires.

🐾 With endless love, zoomies, and slightly manipulative puppy eyes,
🐾 *Phil the Pug* 🐾

126

📖 From Mama Kaz – With Love & Gratitude

No great story is written alone.

This book is not just a collection of stories—it is a celebration of love, laughter, and the incredible bond we share with the dogs who change our lives.

To Tina & Ezra—You are my heart, my world, my reason for everything. Without you, life wouldn't be the same—you are my loves, my inspiration and my strength. Thank you for being the best part of this journey, for loving Phil, and all the support and inspiration for this book, and for making every day as fun as we can, I love you completely.

🐾 To Phil – Our Little Legend

Phil, our beautiful, mischievous, endlessly lovable pug son, from the moment you arrived, our world changed.

We never could have imagined just how much you would brighten our lives, how deeply your puggy charm, unwavering loyalty, and ridiculous but wonderful antics would fill our days with laughter, love, and pure happiness.

You are more than a pet, more than a companion. You are a force of joy.

You have given us unconditional love the kind that wraps around our hearts and refuses to let go. You have taught us that life should be full of cuddles, zoomies, and the occasional well-planned snack heist.

You have entertained us, protected us, reminded us that true love is felt in every little moment—the way you look at us, the way you trust us, the way you choose to be by our side, always.

Phil, you are a legend in your own right. And we are eternally grateful for every single moment with you. We love you.

To Froggo, Pumpkin, and Nanny Hannah—For bringing Phil into this world, for caring for him before we knew him, for making sure he arrived ready to love, to laugh, to steal snacks with pure determination.

To Zachary & Saffron—For tolerating the presence of an overly enthusiastic pug, for entertaining him even when you pretend not to, for being a part of this little family in your own unique way.

🐾 **To Mylo & Mas Boutique**: A special thank you to **Mylo & Mas Boutique**, for bringing Phil into their world and giving him a place in their incredible brand. From the thoughtful designs to the outstanding quality, every piece has made Phil's adventures extra stylish and comfortable. **Mylo, Martina, and Michaela**—Your dedication, creativity, and kindness shine through everything you do, and we are so grateful for the love and support you've shown Phil.

🐾 **To Phil's Instagram crew**—Mylo Murphy, Harry, Murphy, Idah-Rose, Dave Puggo, Sammy, Barry, Duckie, Tofu, Mase, James, Teddy, Frankie, Jack, Sir Jeeves, Mousey, in fact all of you following Phil— your friendships mean the world to him, and to us. You've built something special, something joyful. Thank you for being a huge part of our journey and an inspiration for this book!

With love, gratitude, and endless pug cuddles,

Mama Kaz.

www.ingramcontent.com/pod-product-compliance
Lightning Source LLC
Chambersburg PA
CBHW051320120626
46547CB00015B/2324